Winter / Christmas Coloring Book

Adult Coloring Books

Aryla Publishing 2019

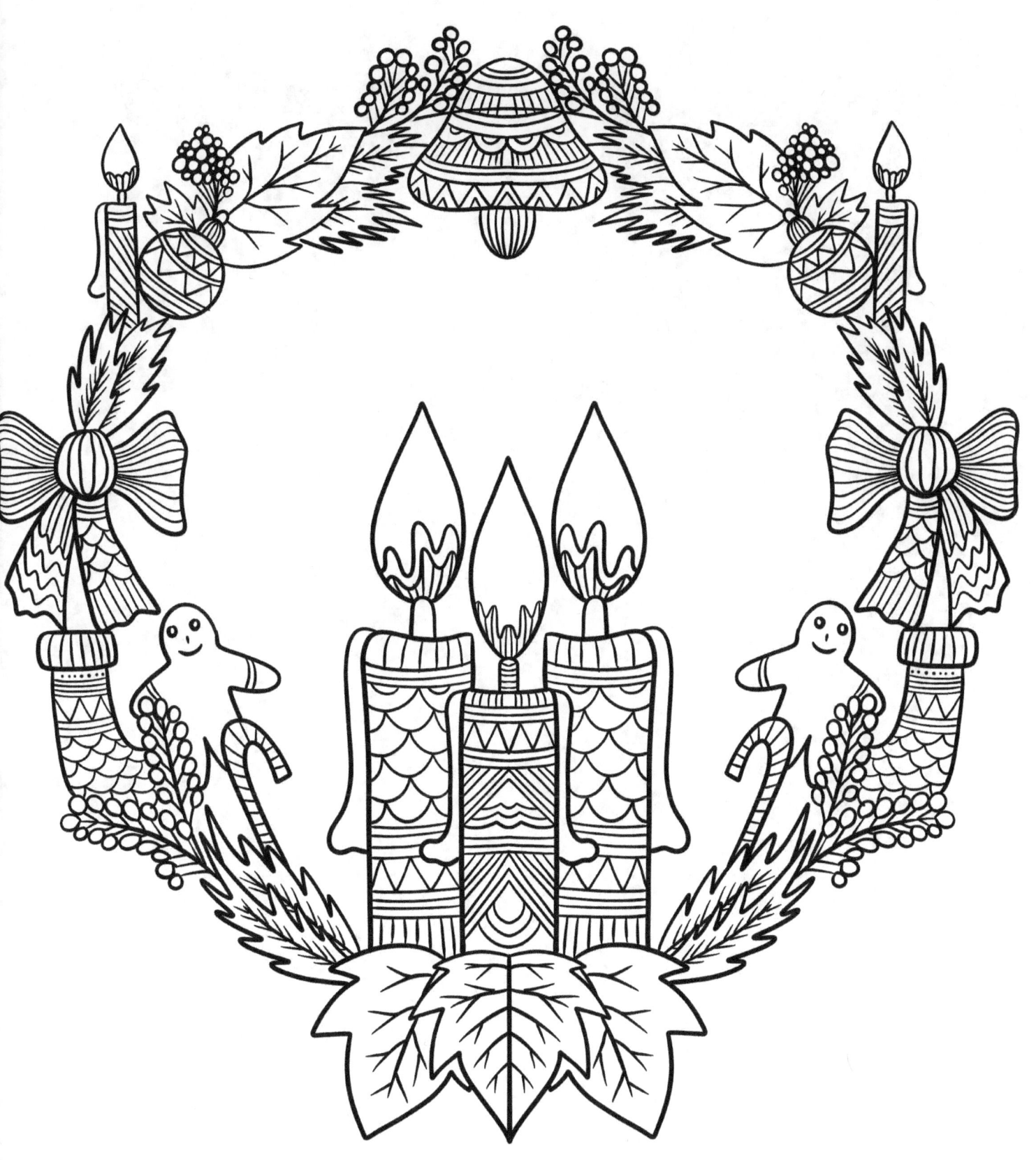

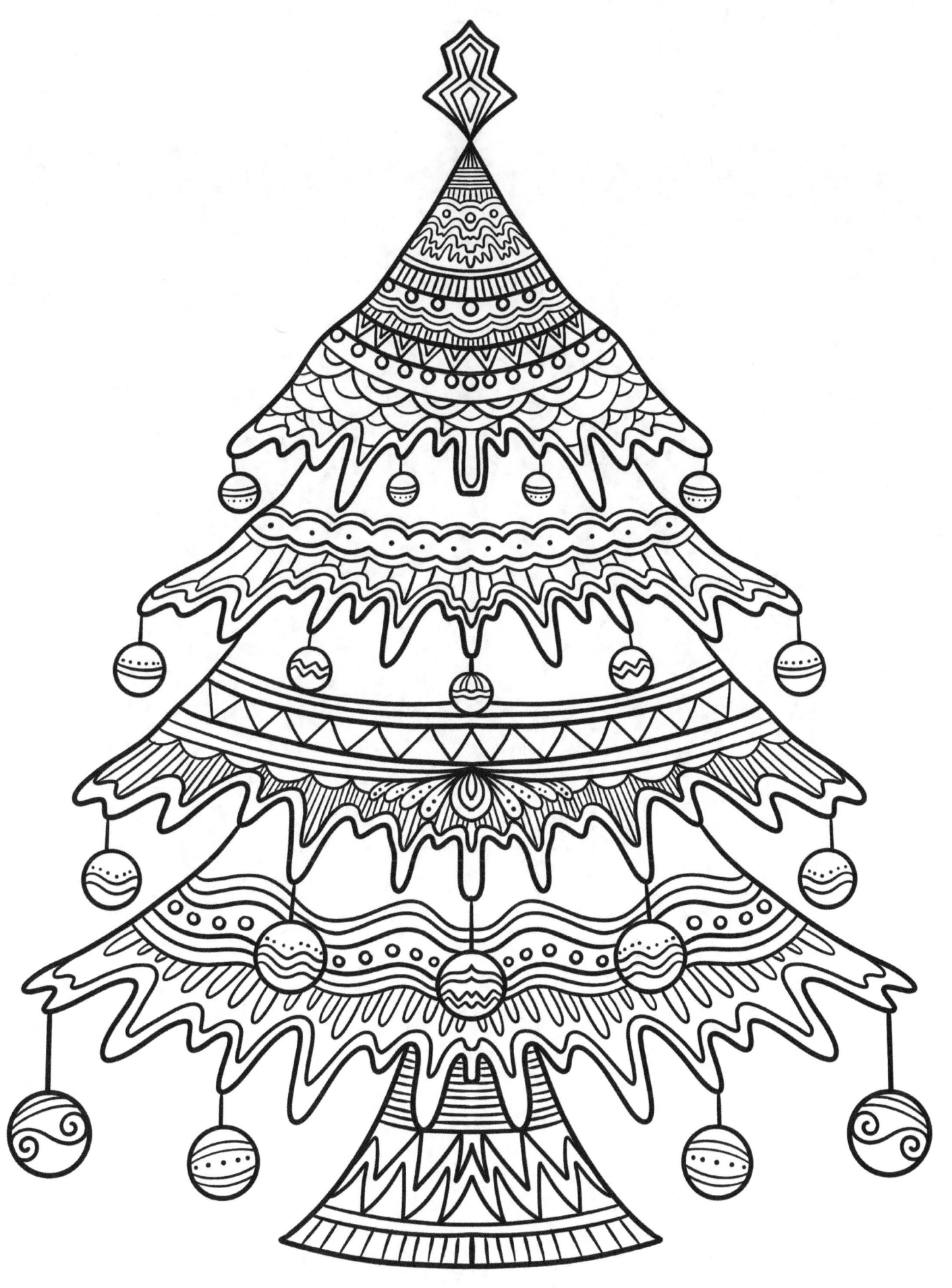

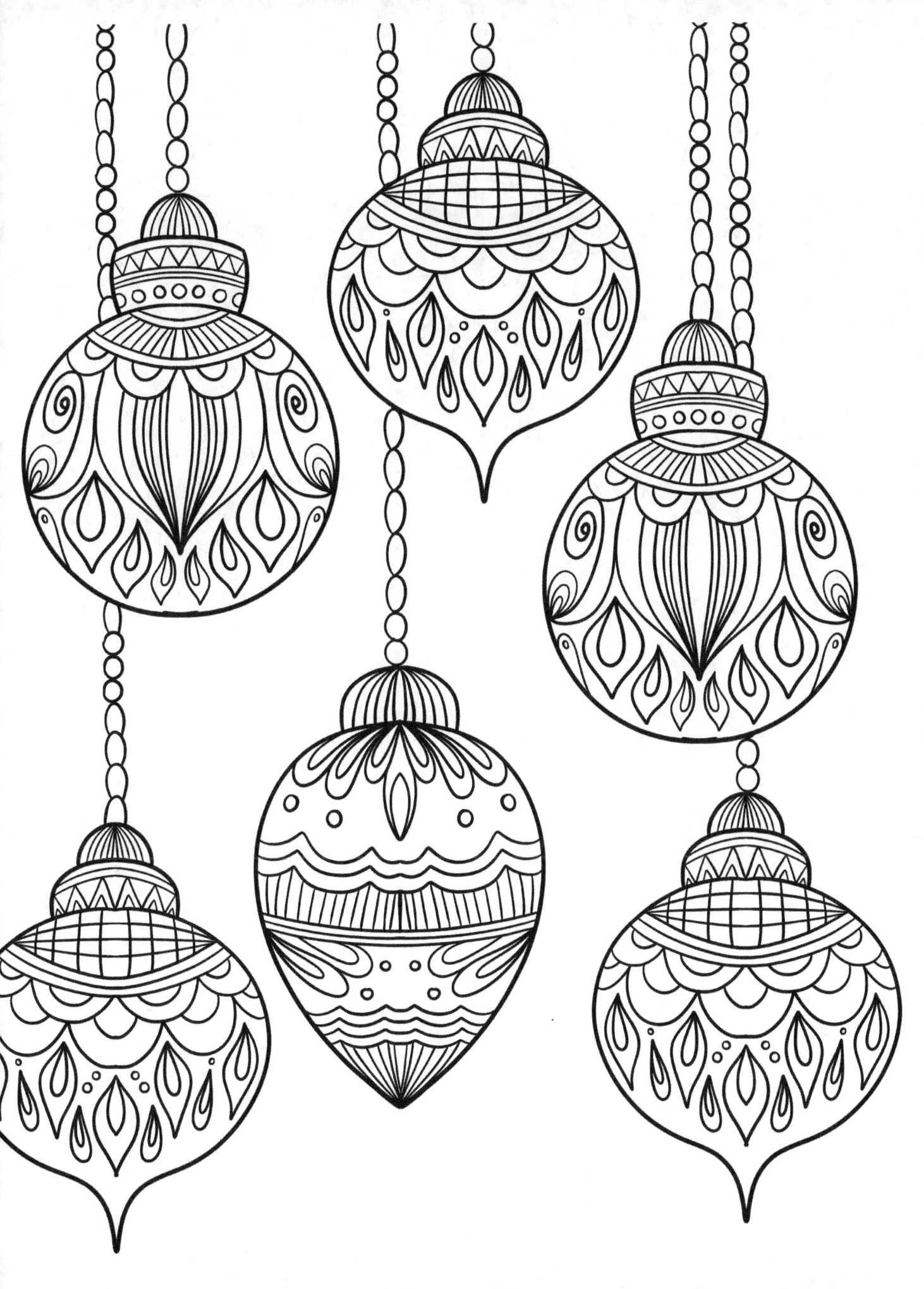

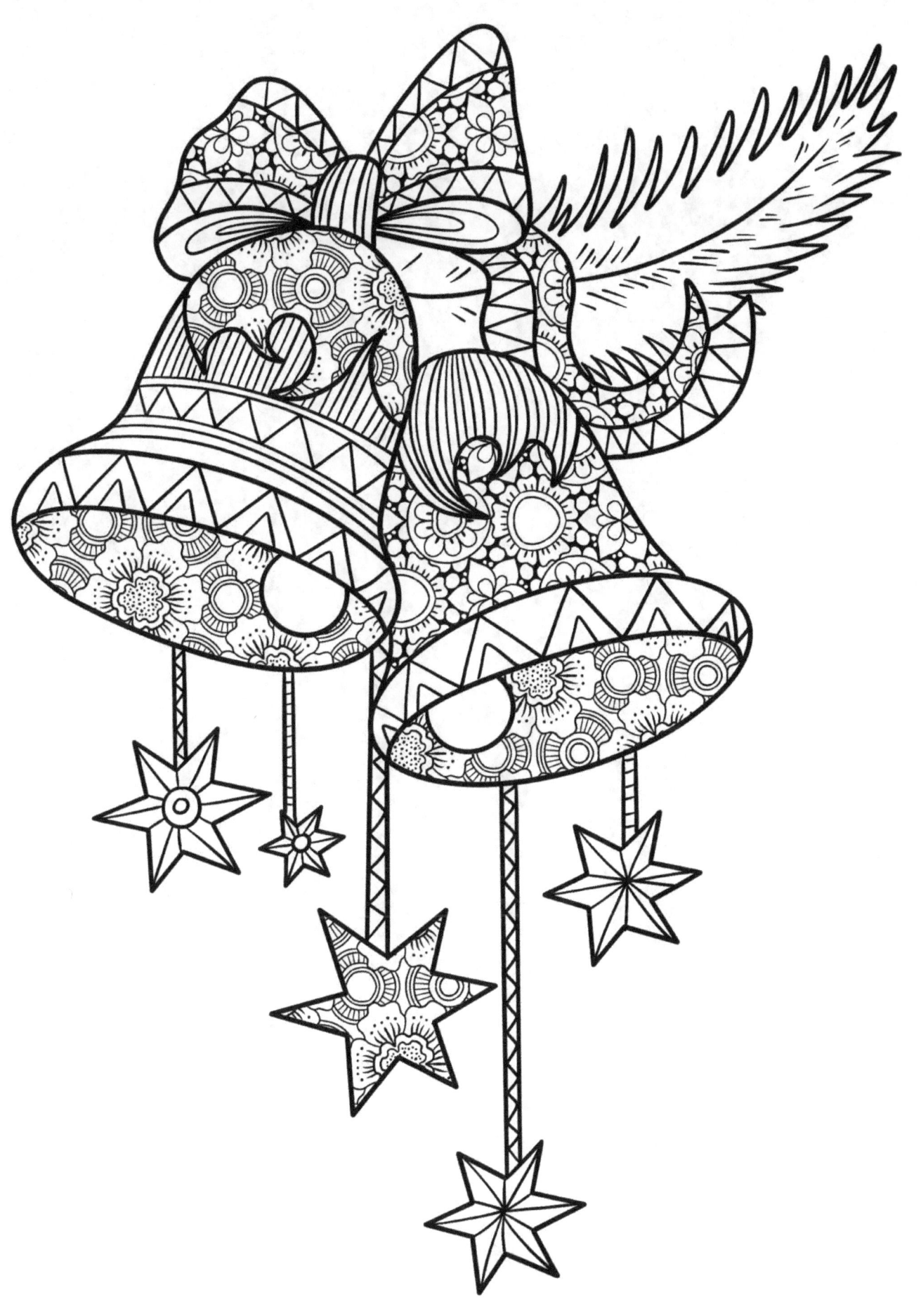

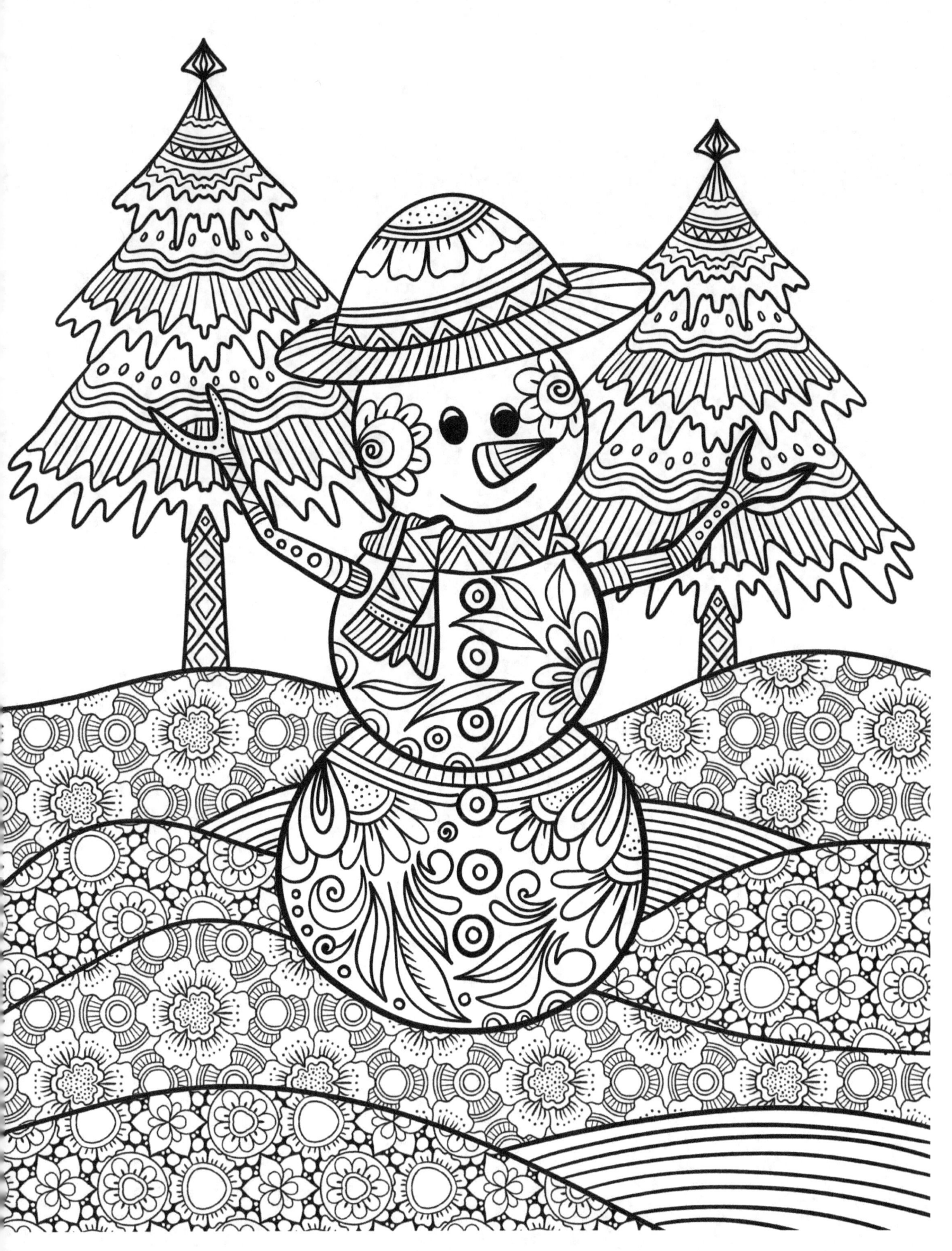

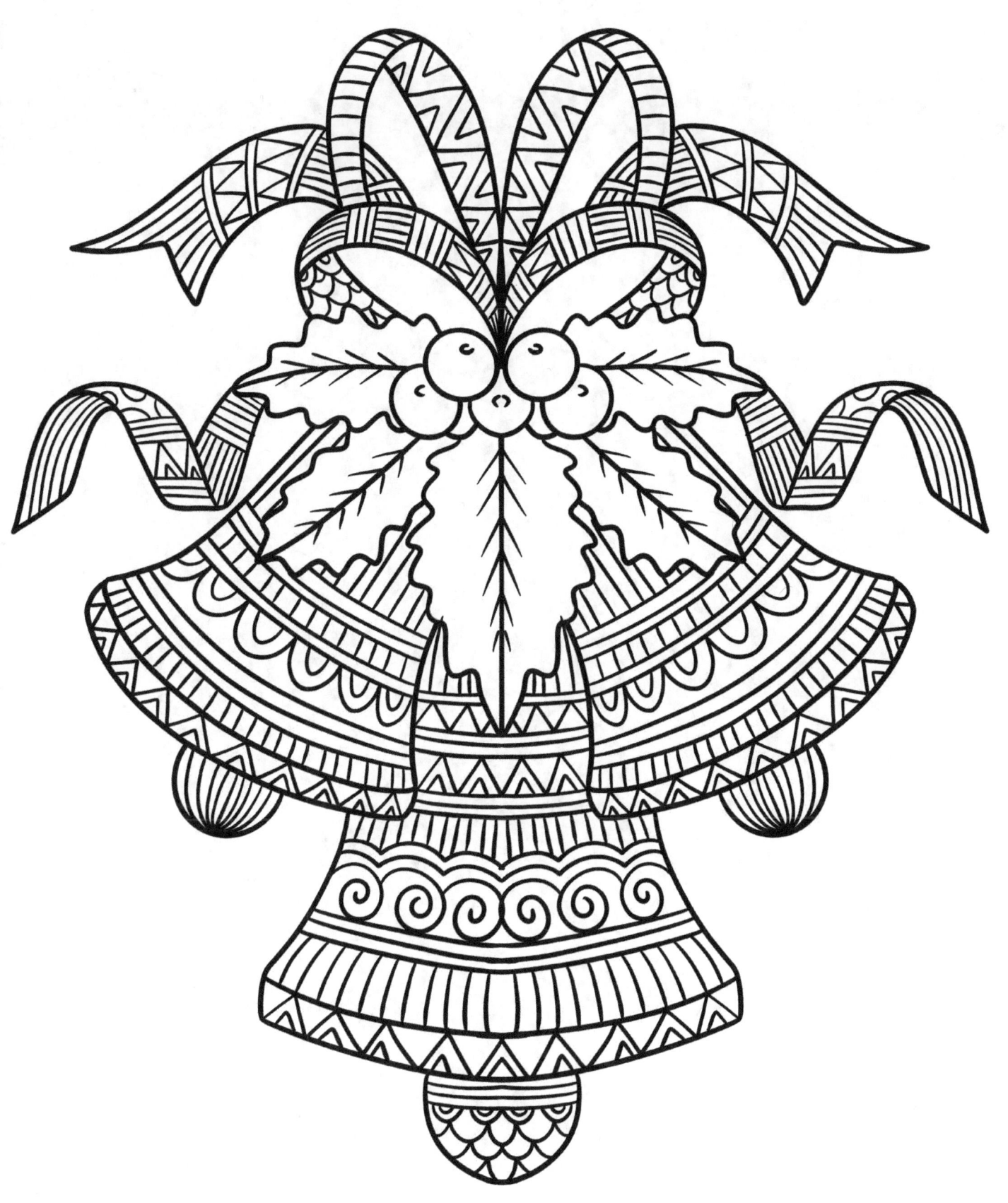

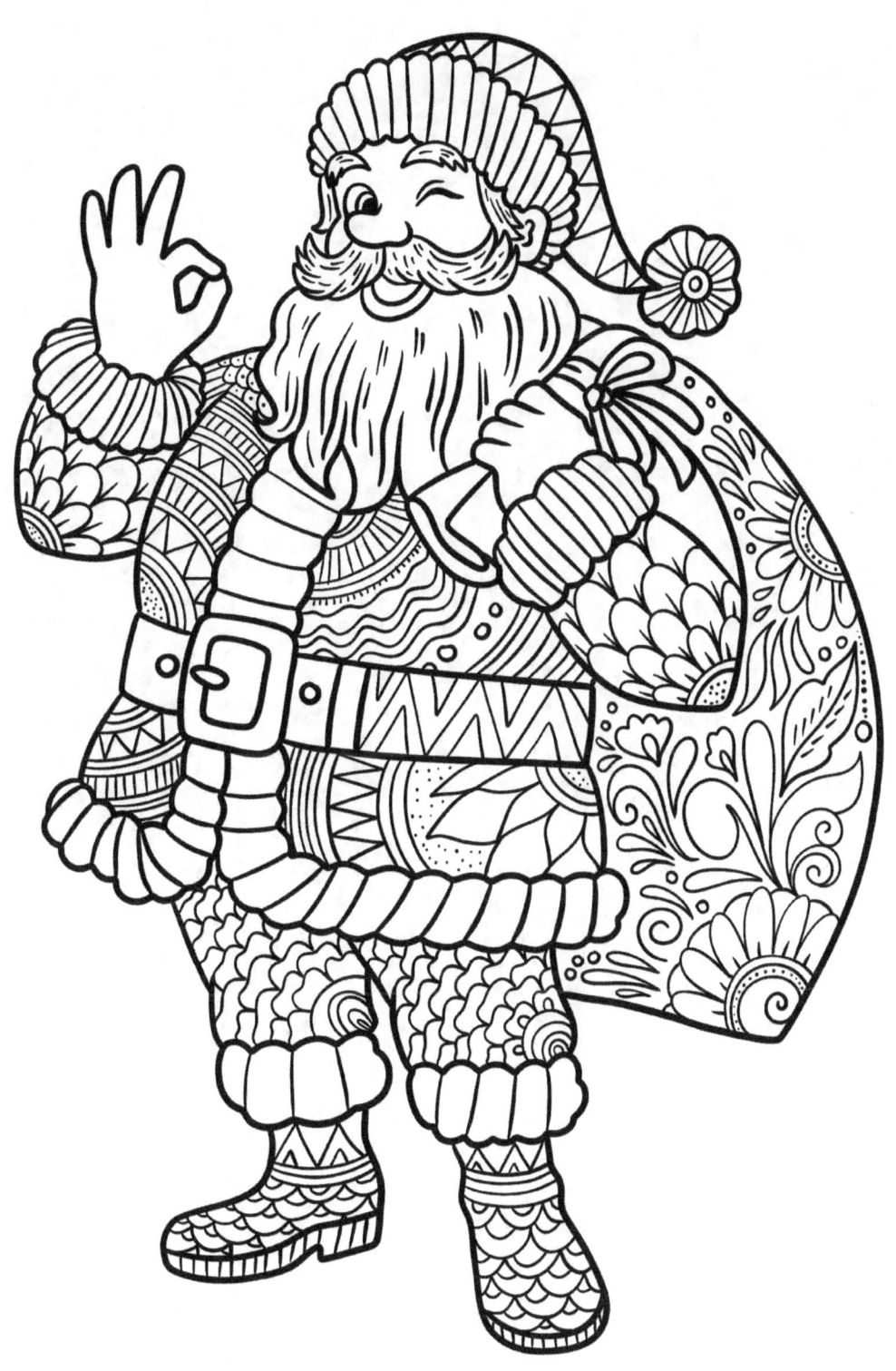

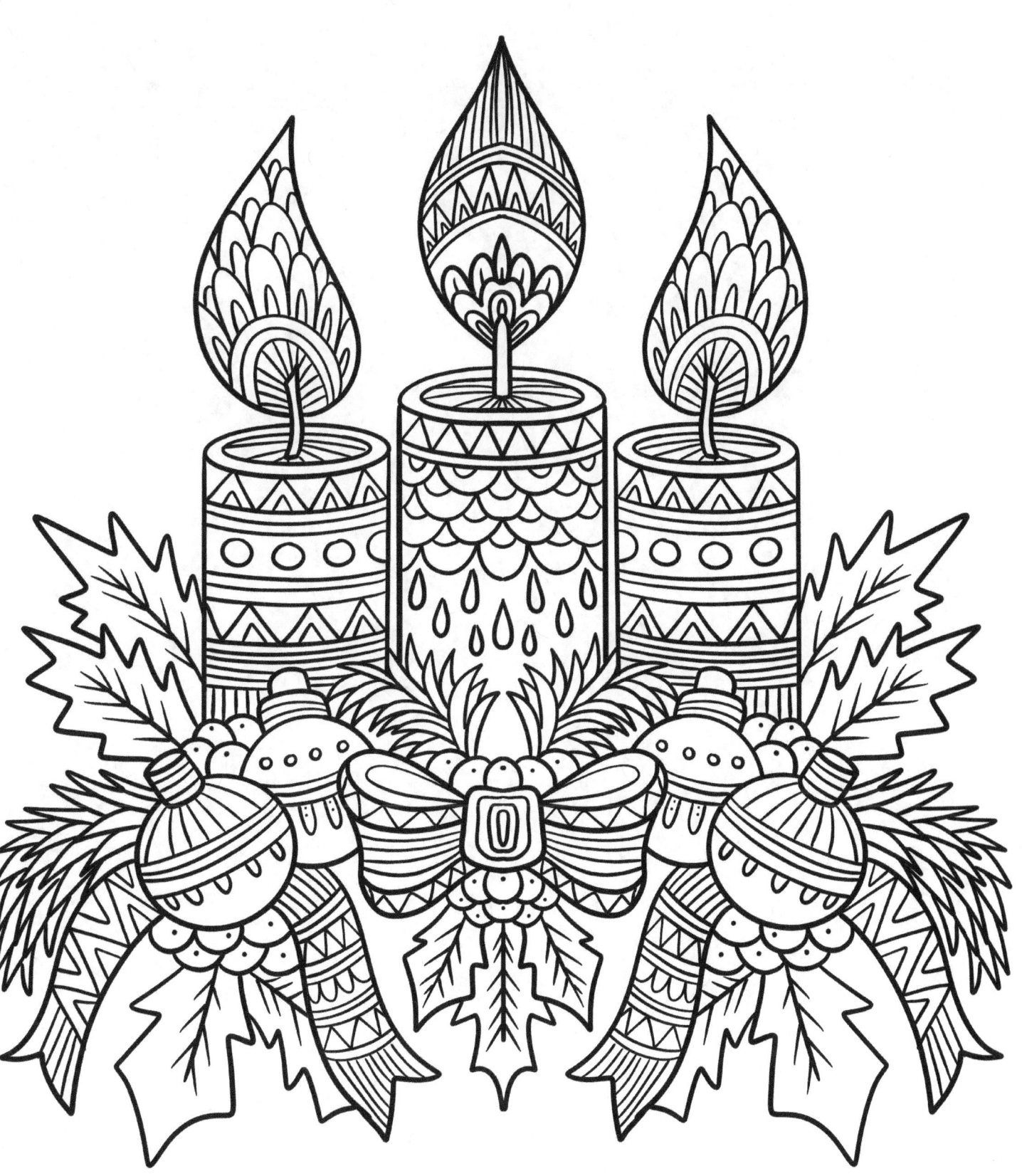

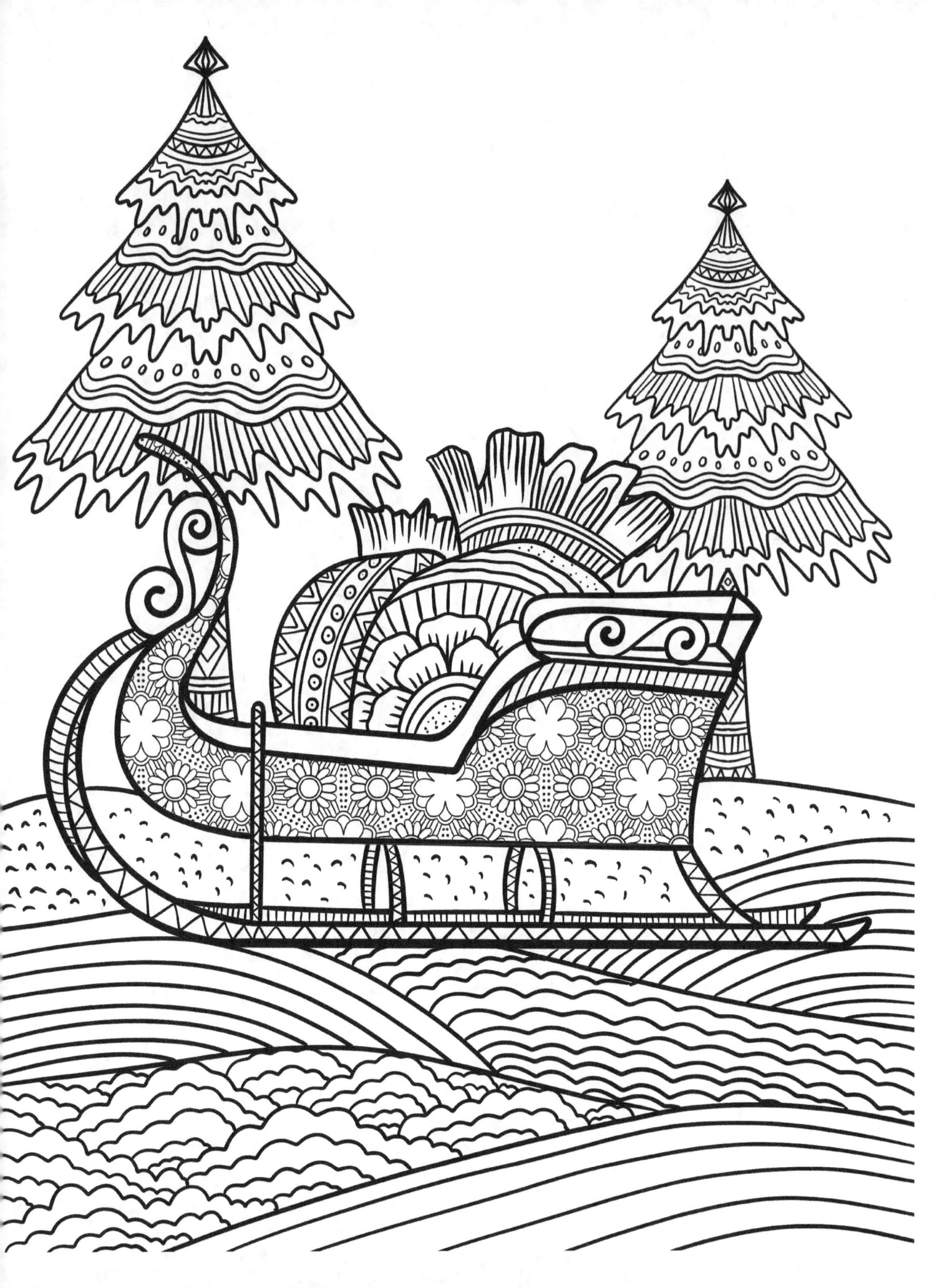

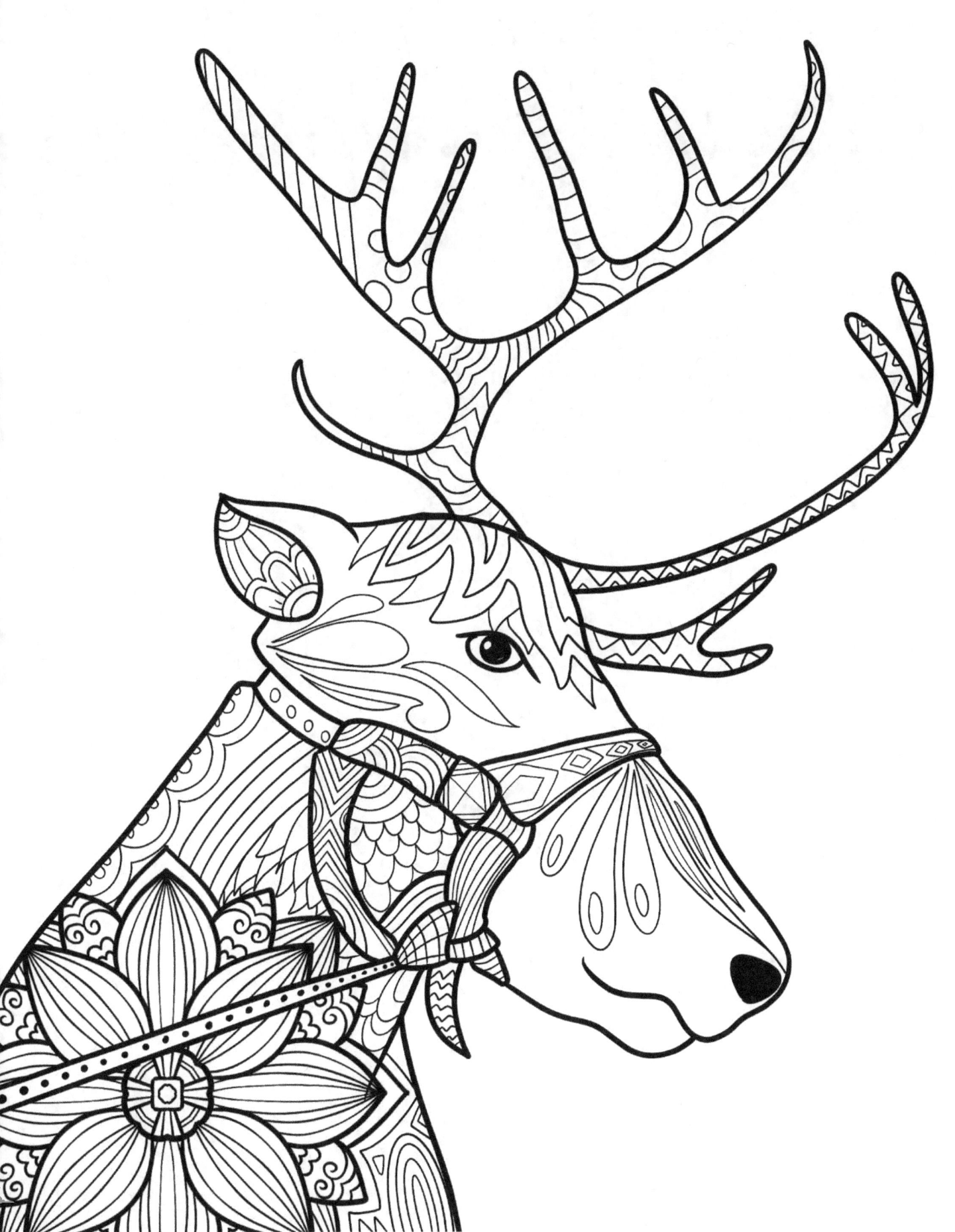

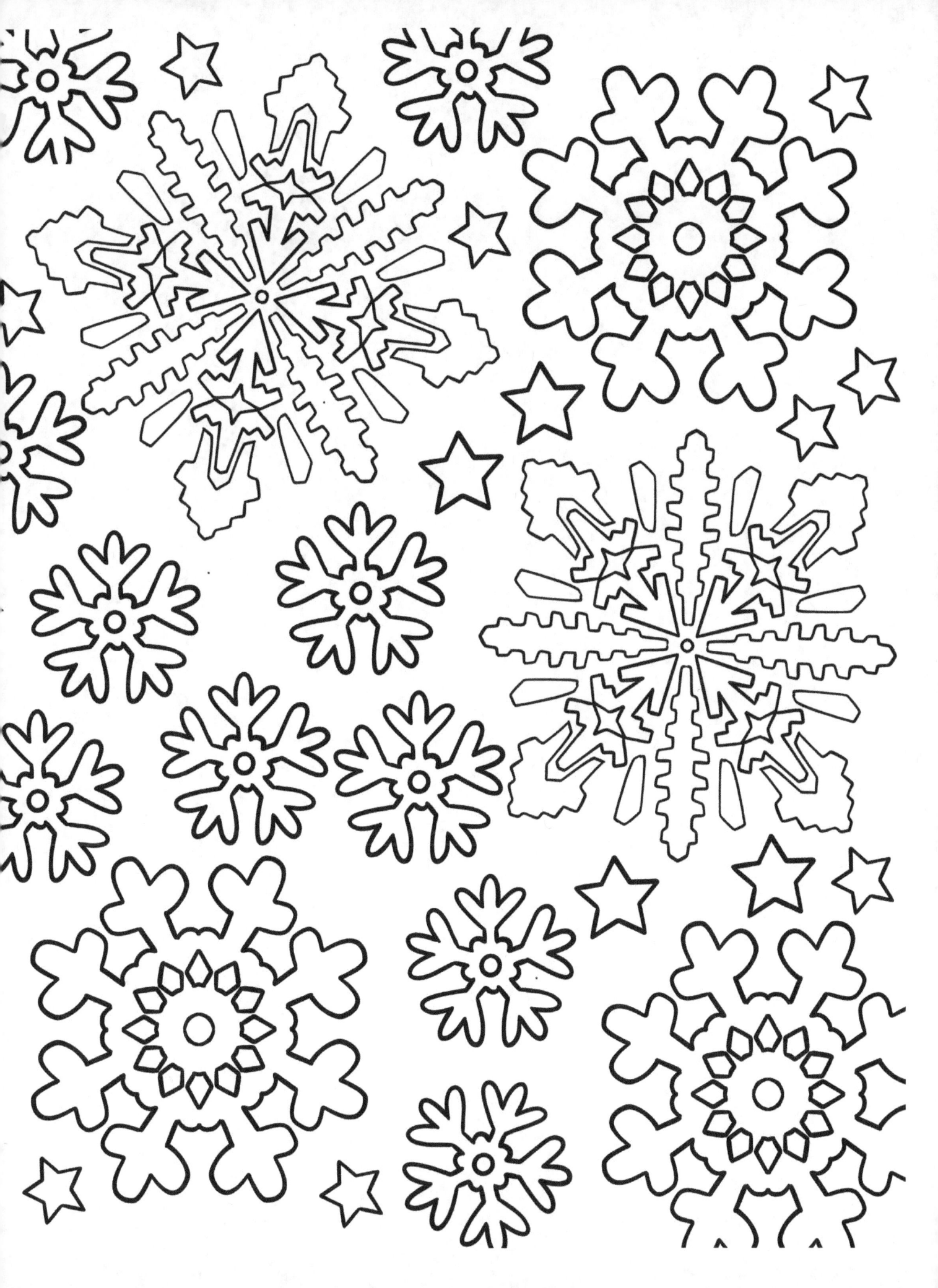

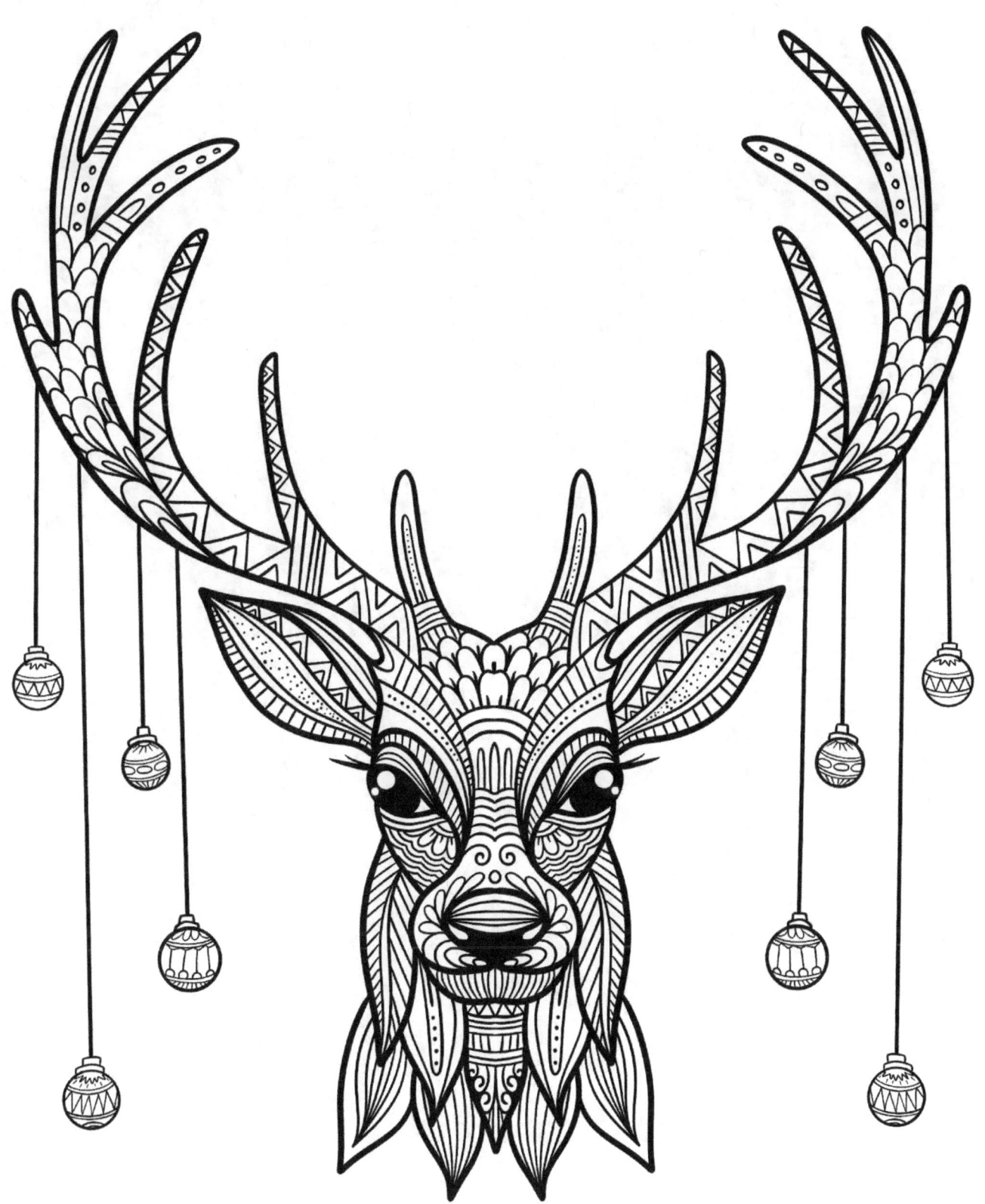

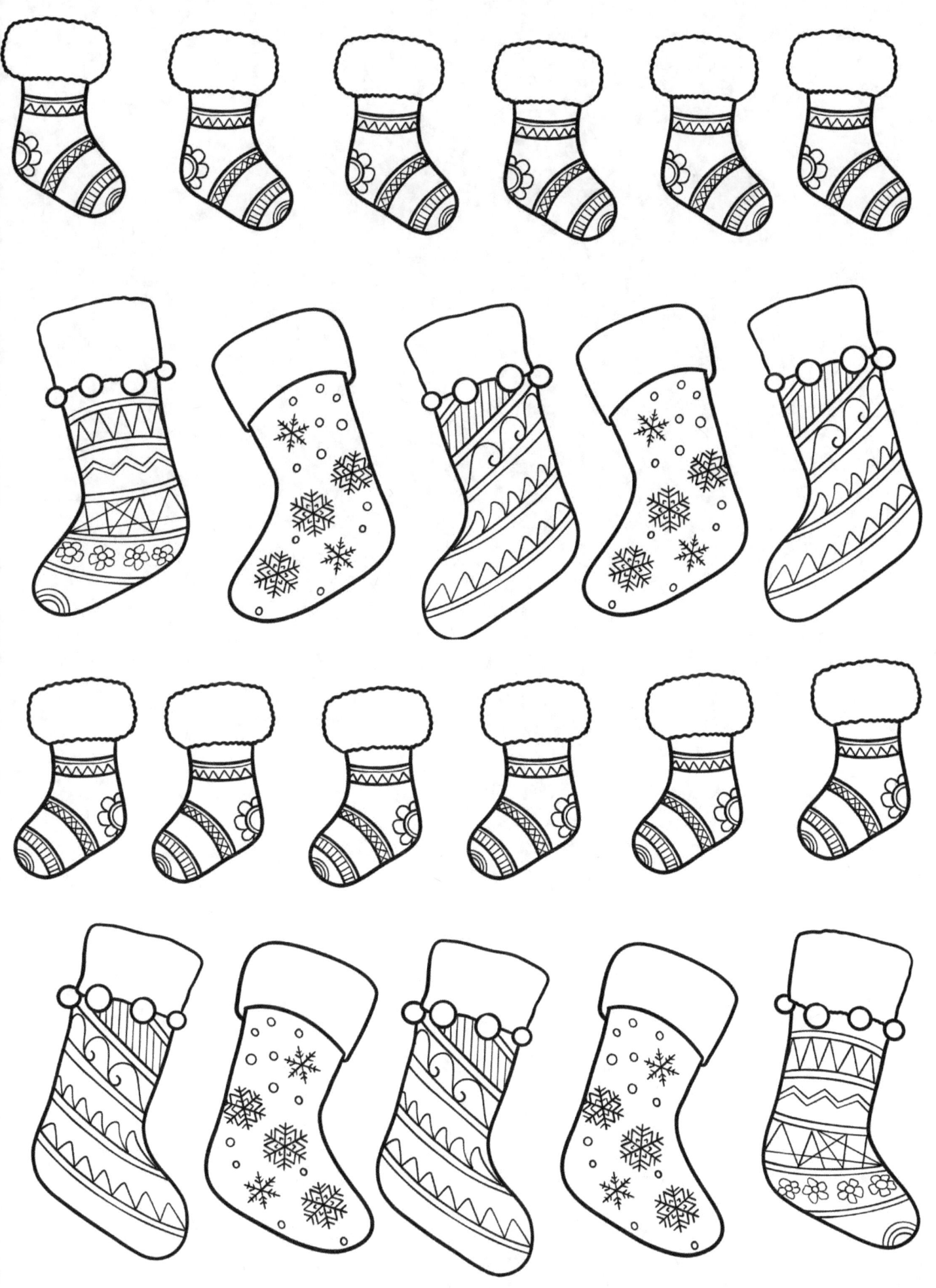

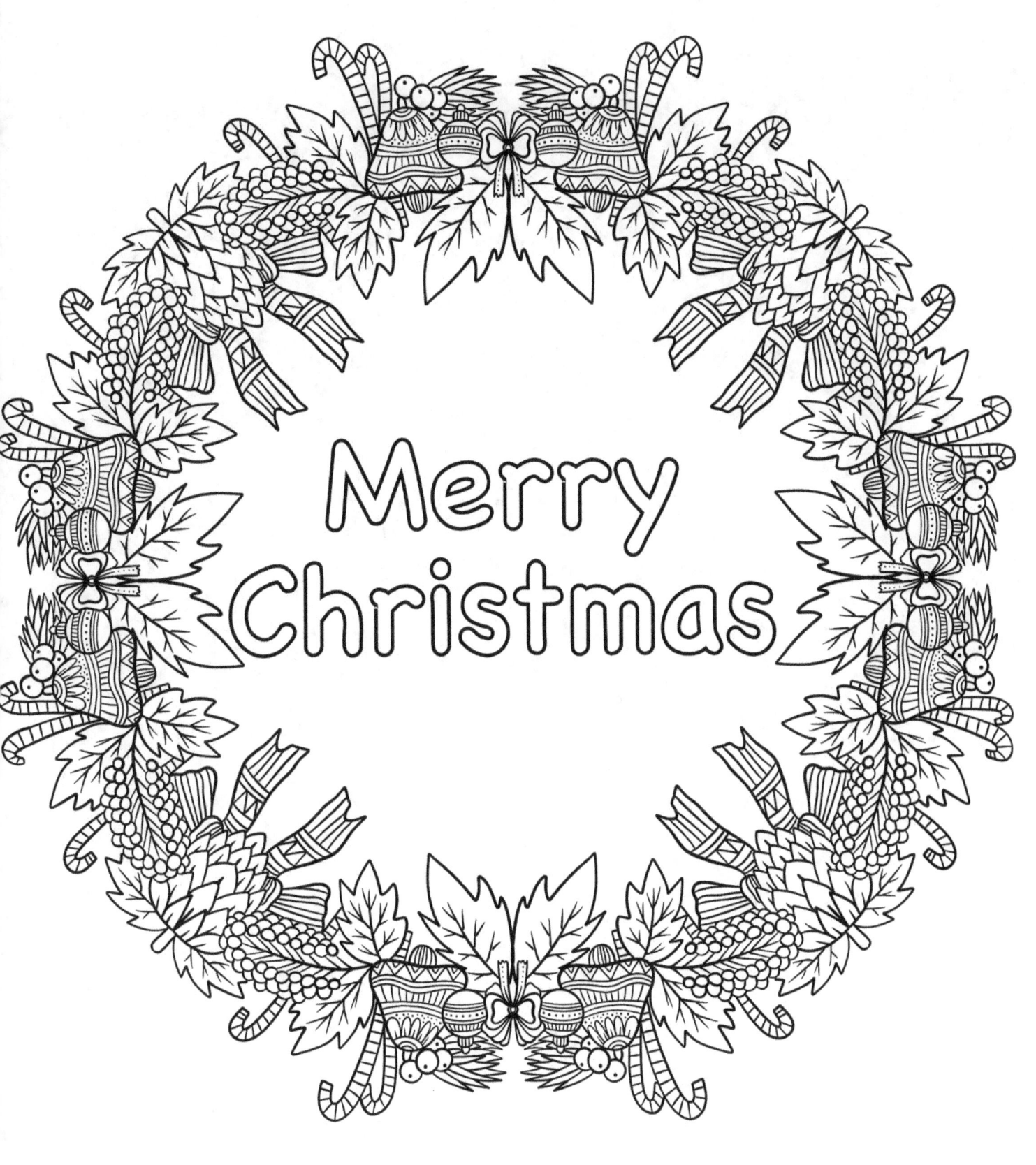

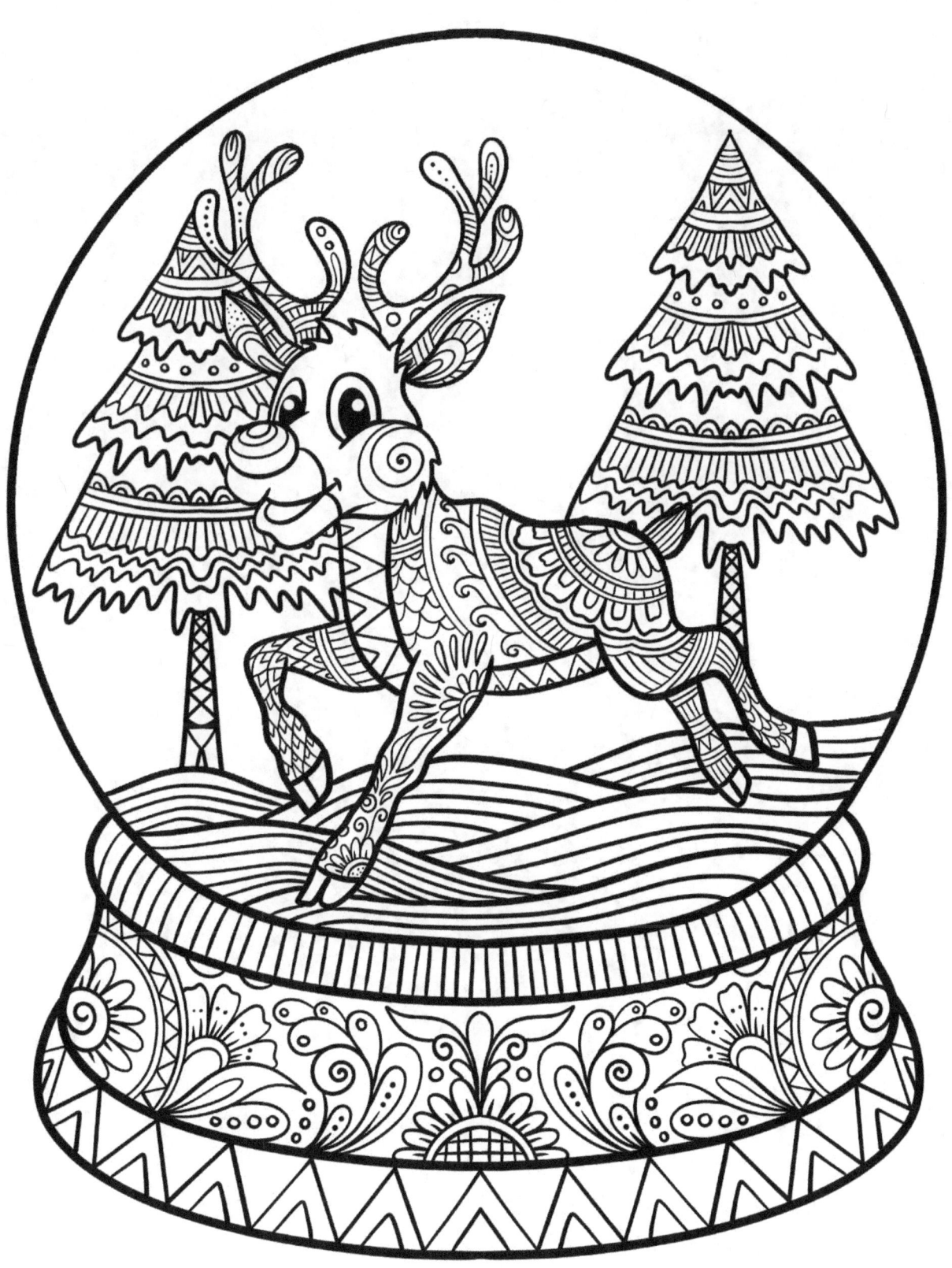

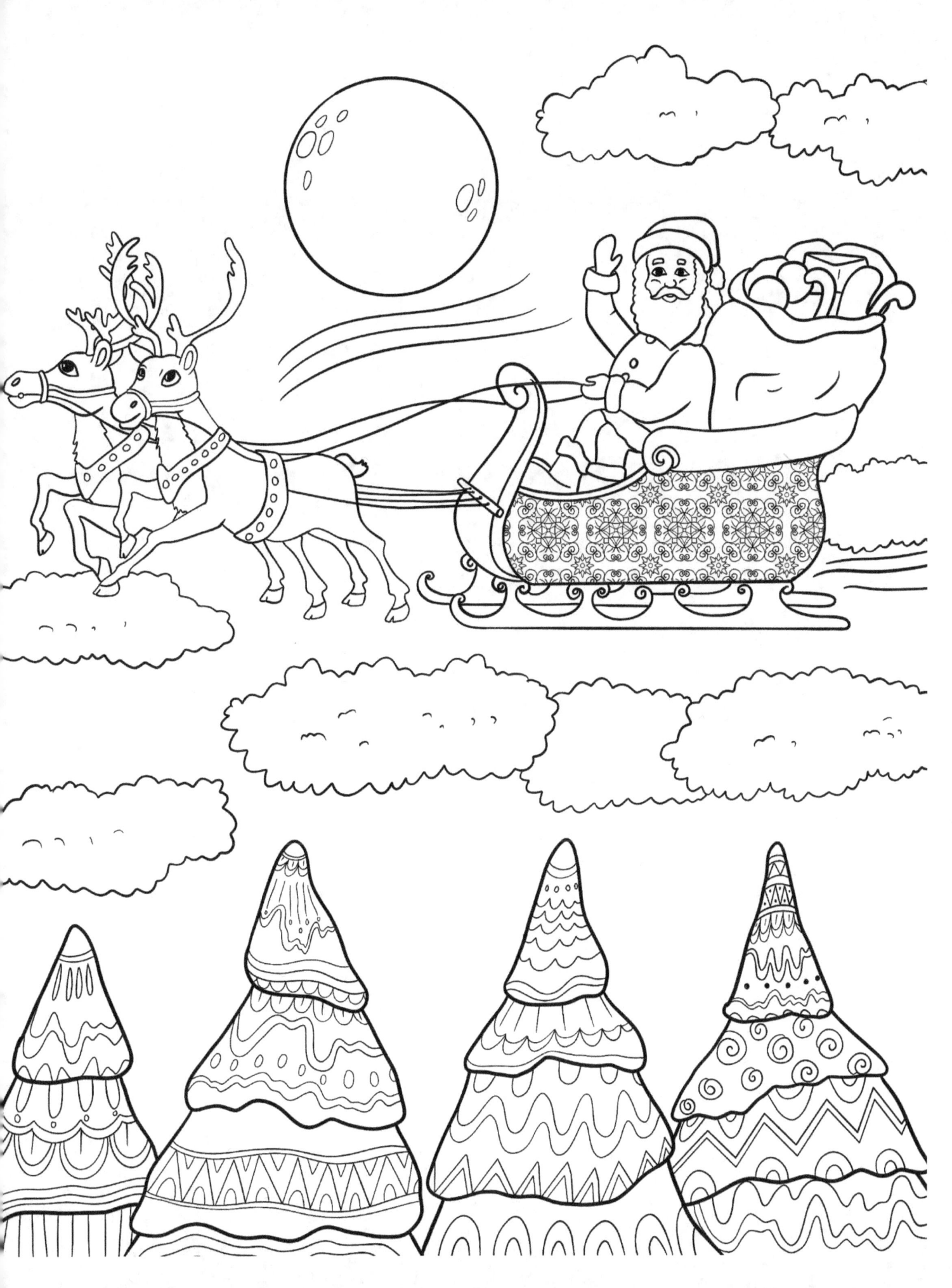

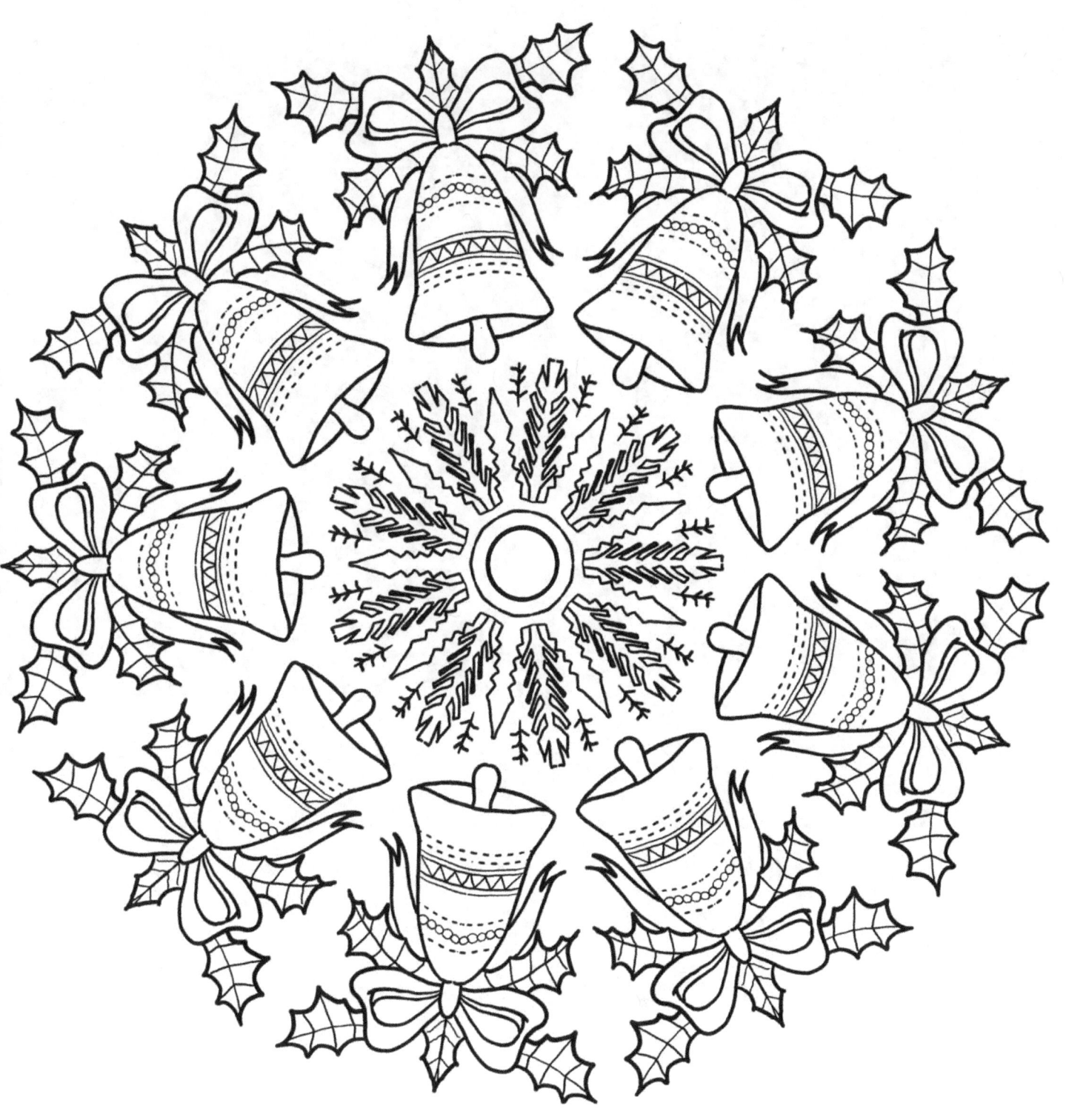

Merrry Christmas ....!!

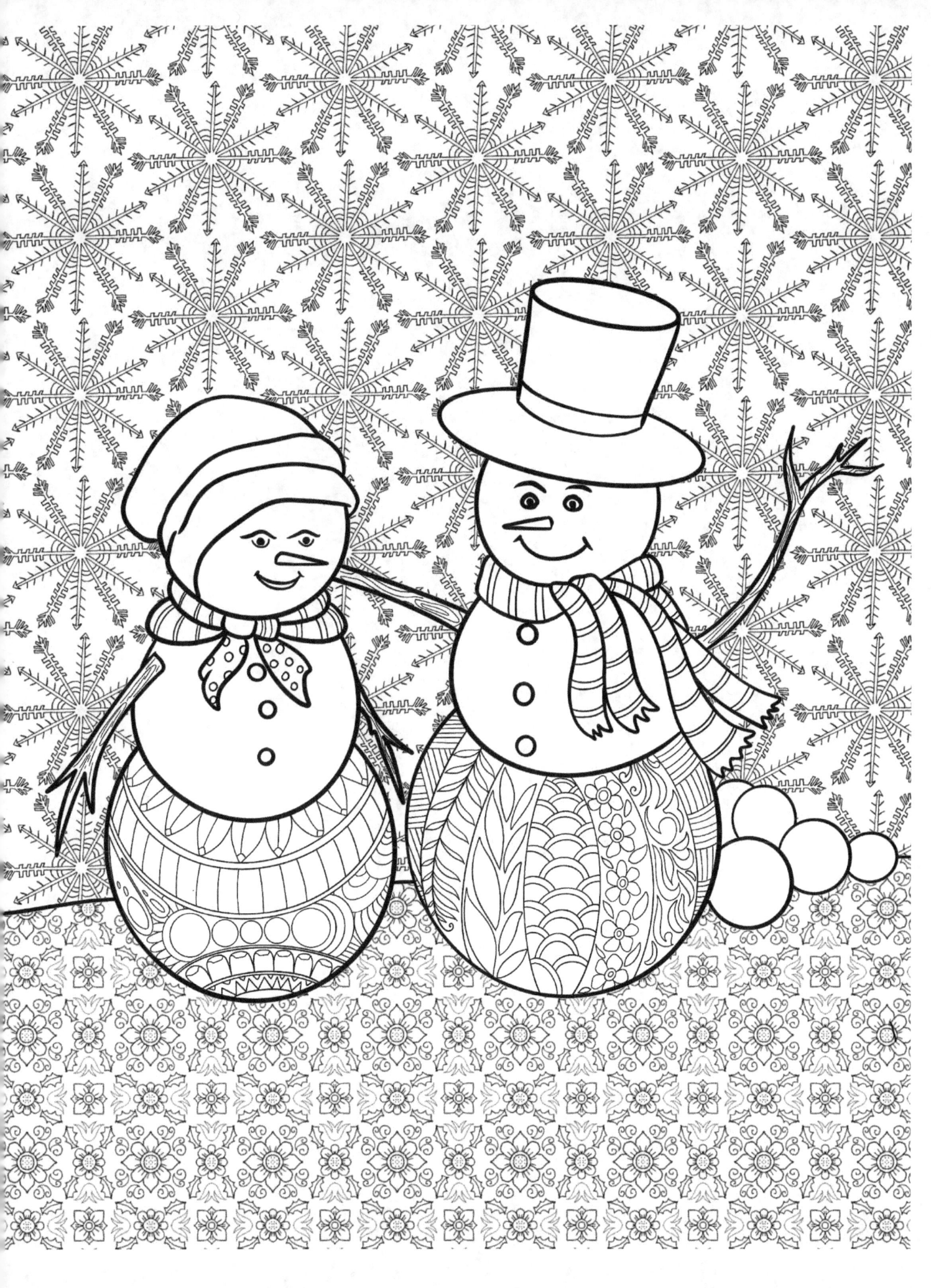

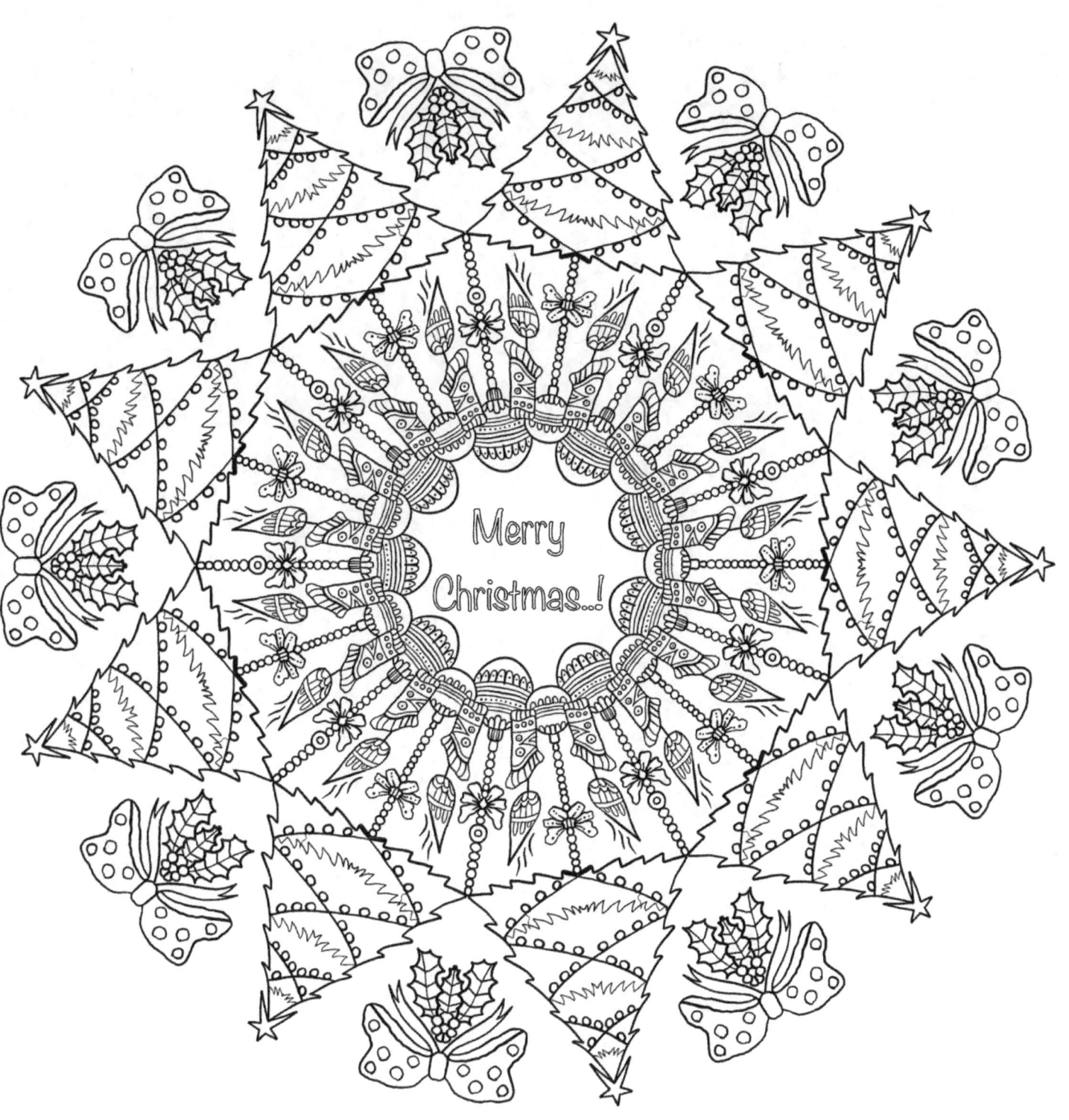

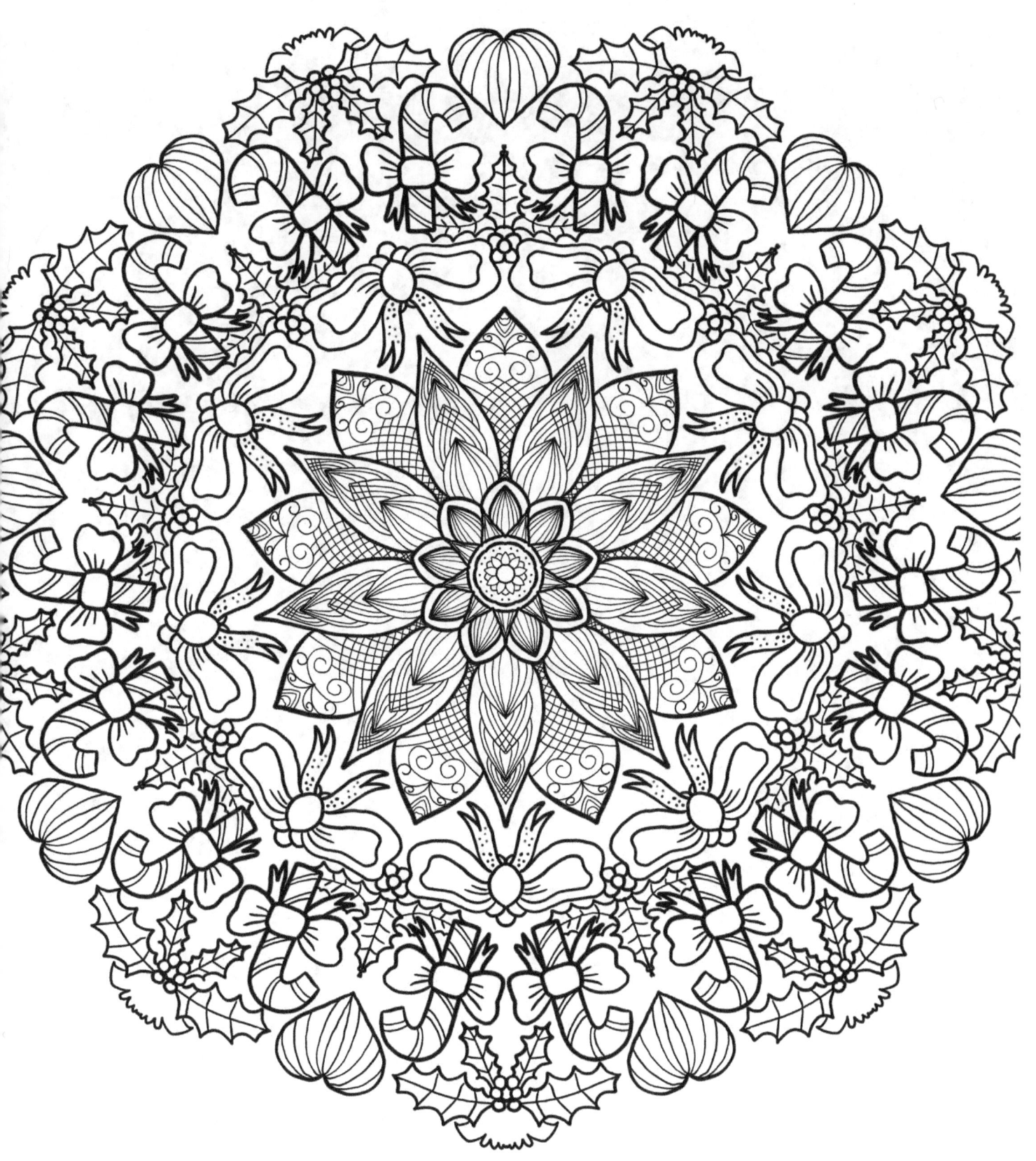

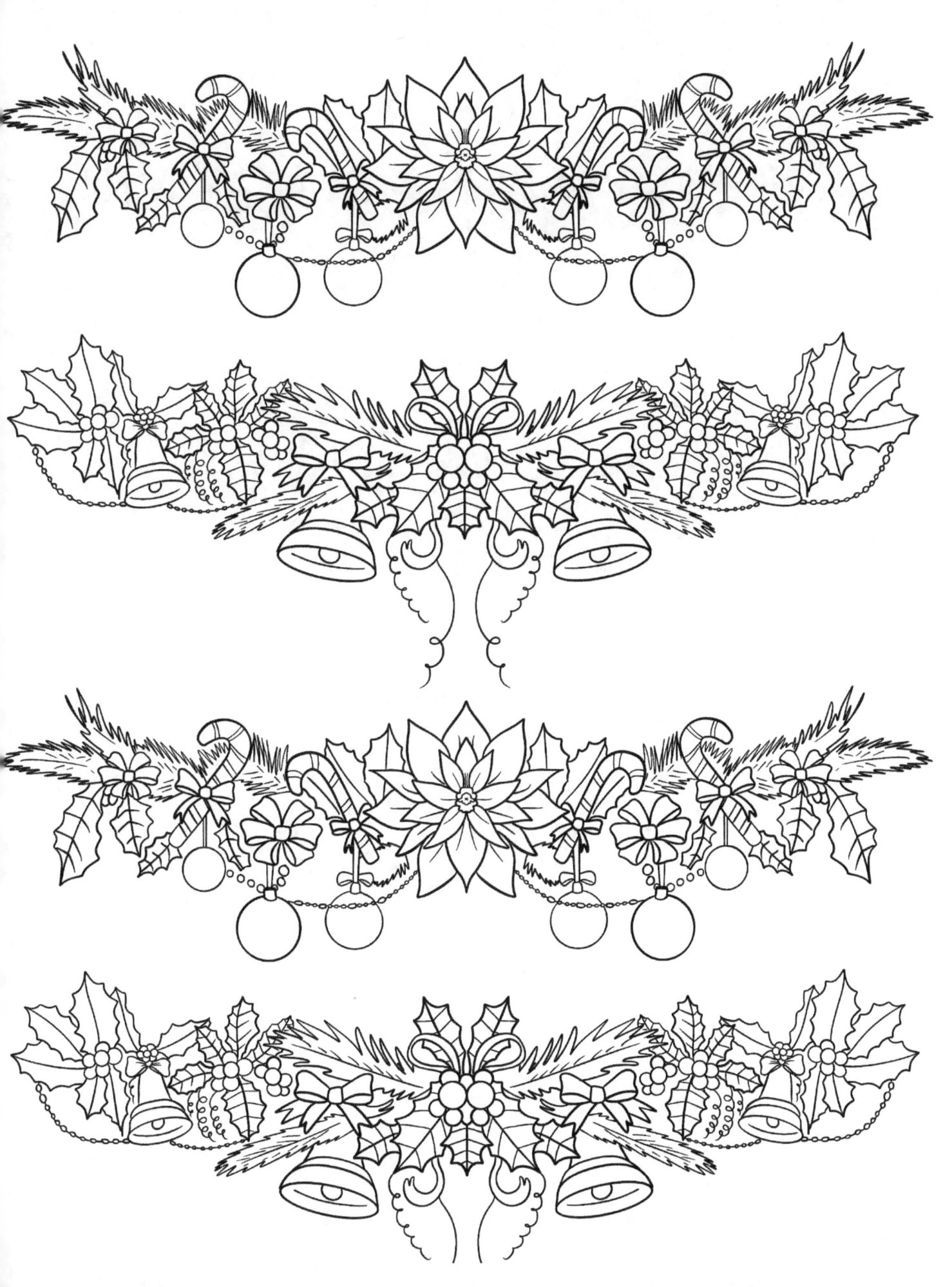

Other Coloring Books from Aryla Publishing

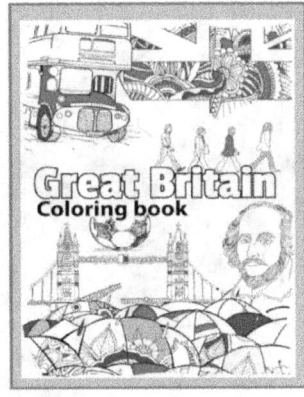
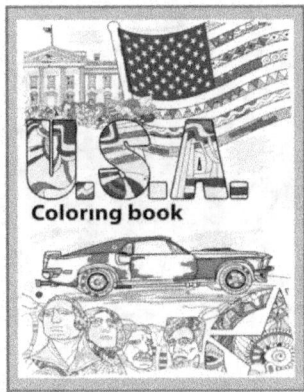
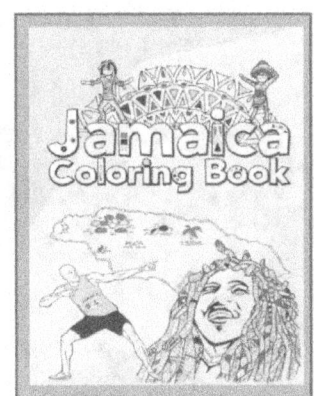
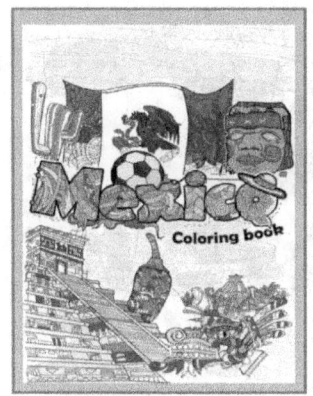

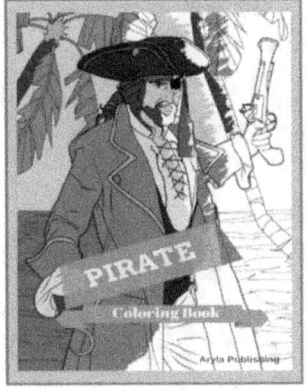
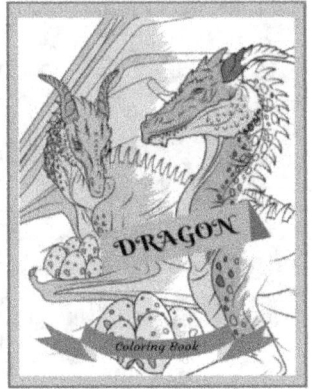
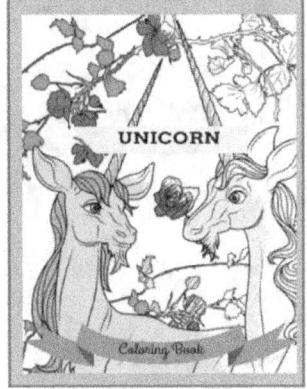
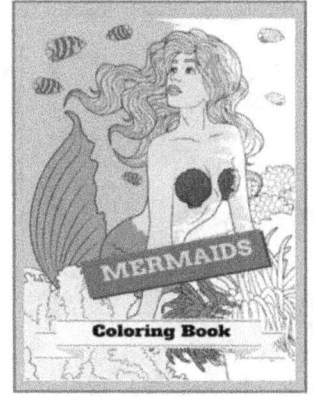

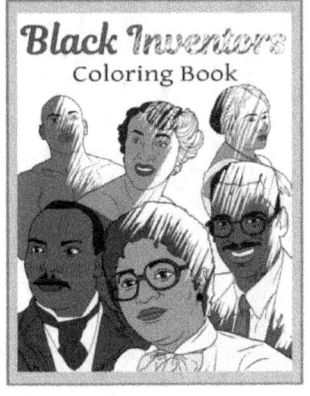
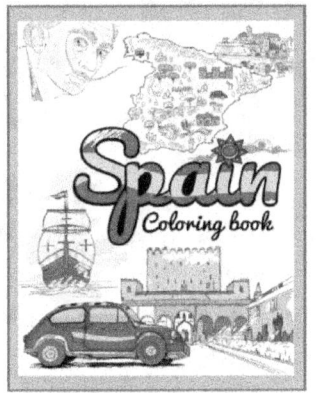
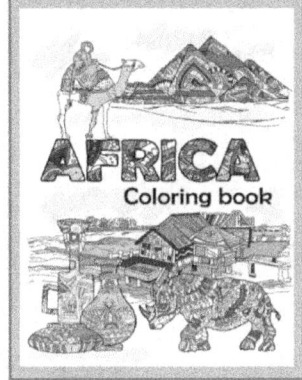
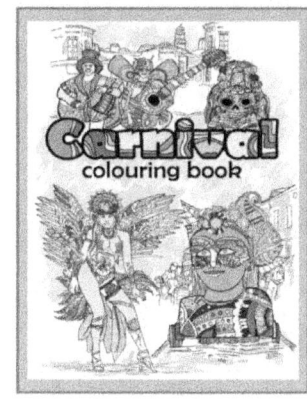

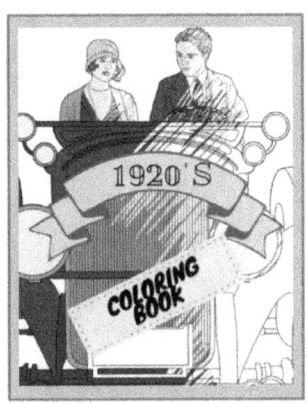
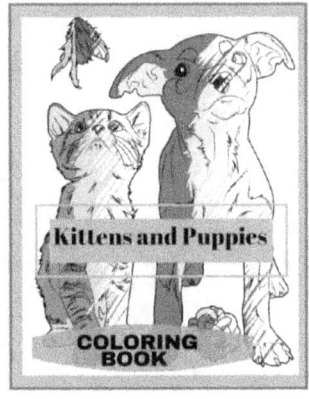
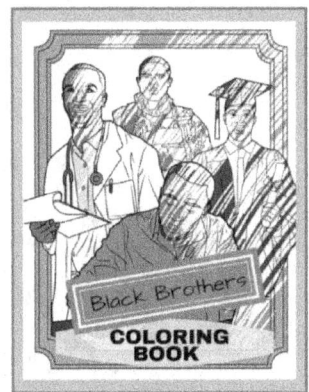
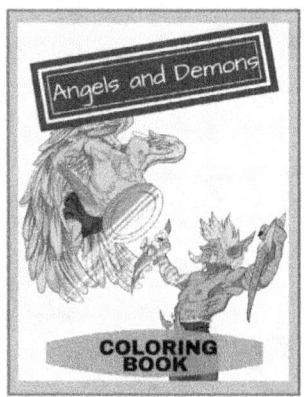

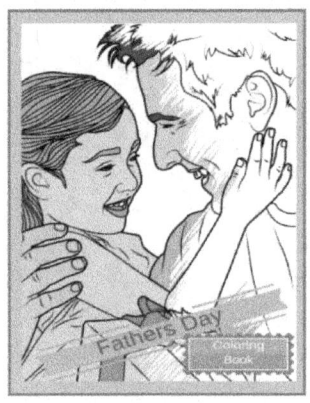
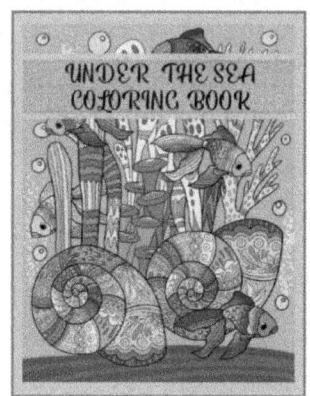
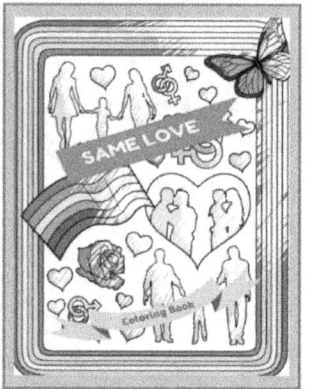
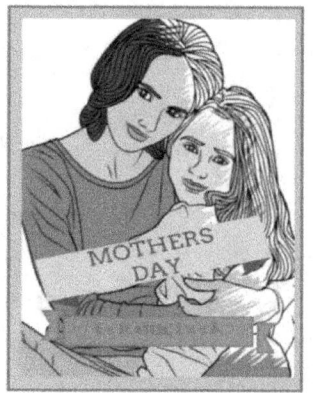
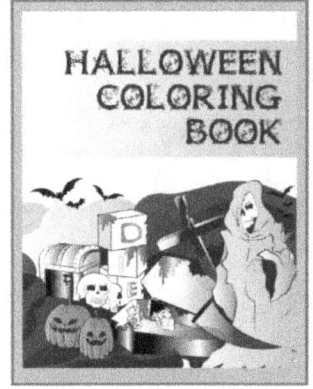
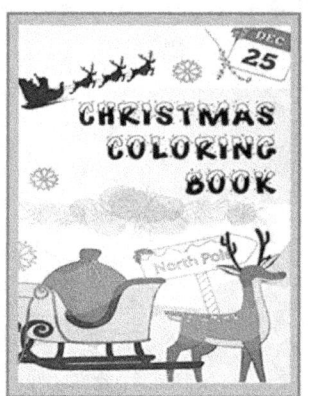
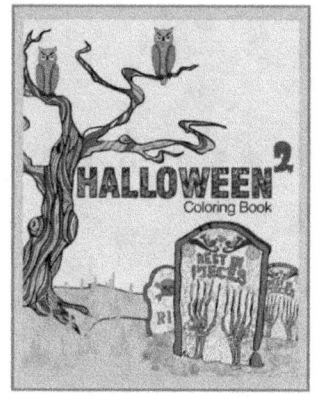
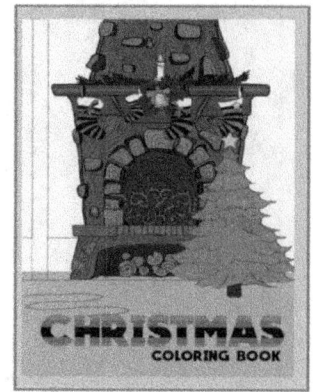
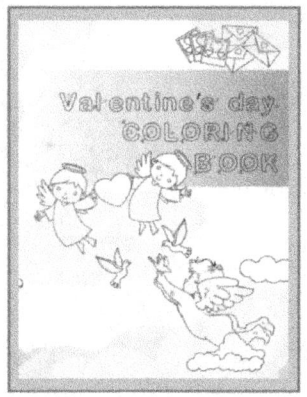
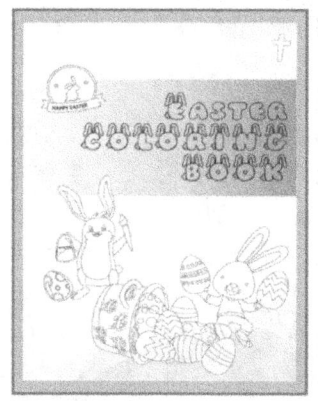
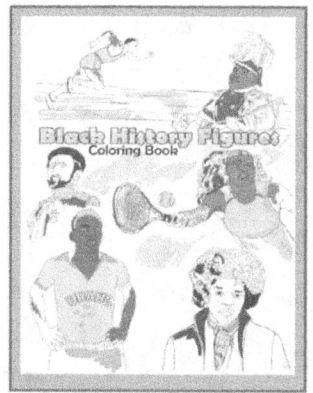

Thank you for purchasing this book.

If you would like to know more about Aryla Publishing Books please visit:-

www.ArylaPublishing.com

Or follow us on
Facebook
Twitter
Instagram
for *free promotions*

@arylapublishing

We would love to know what you think of this book so please leave us a review.

Have a wonderful day ☺

Visit **www.ArylaPublishing.com**
to find out about all new releases.

Follow us @arylapublishing on Twitter Instagram & Facebook

Search for Aryla Publishing on

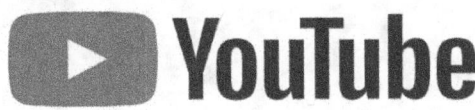 YouTube

Check out our <u>Book Trailers</u>

<u>Subscribe</u> to keep up to date with new releases!

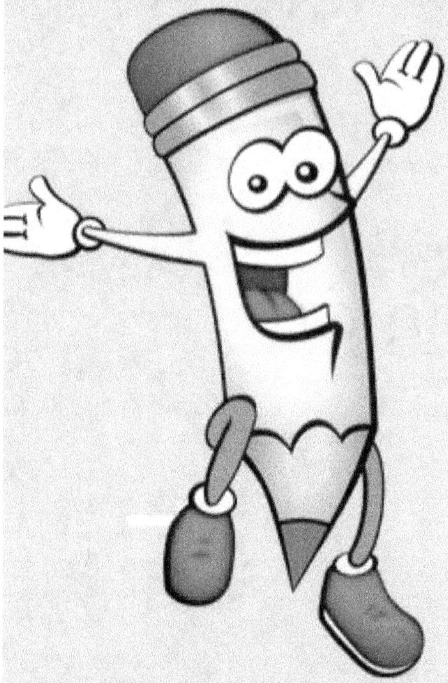

WE WOULD LOVE YOUR FEEDBACK

PLEASE LEAVE REVIEW AT:-

www.ingramcontent.com/pod-product-compliance
Lightning Source LLC
Chambersburg PA
CBHW080136240526
45468CB00009BA/2466

* 9 7 8 1 9 1 2 6 7 5 5 6 2 *